Kṛṣṇa, the Reservoir of Pleasure

HIS DIVINE GRACE
A.C. BHAKTIVEDANTA SWAMI PRABHUPĀDA

FOUNDER-ĀCĀRYA OF THE INTERNATIONAL SOCIETY FOR KRISHNA CONSCIOUSNESS

contents

Kṛṣṇa, the Reservoir of Pleasure   6

Kṛṣṇa, the Supreme Lovable Object   19

The Perfect Person   24

Readers interested in the subject matter of this pamphlet are invited by the International Society for Krishna Consciousness to correspond with its Secretary at one of the following addresses:

International Society for Krishna Consciousness
Vedic Farm Project
Zielberg 20
8391 Jandelsbrunn
West Germany
Tel: 08583-316

International Society for Krishna Consciousness
Almviks gård
153 00 Järna
Sweden
Tel: 0755-52068

Sixth Printing, 1990: 1,000,000
© 1990 The Bhaktivedanta Book Trust
All Rights Reserved
ISBN 0-89213-149-7

His Divine Grace
A.C. Bhaktivedanta Swami Prabhupāda

    Śrīla Prabhupāda left India in 1965, at age sixty-nine, to fulfill his spiritual master's request that he teach the science of Kṛṣṇa consciousness throughout the English-speaking world. In a dozen years he published some seventy volumes of translation and commentary on India's Vedic literature, and these are now standard in universities worldwide. Meanwhile, traveling almost nonstop, Śrīla Prabhupāda molded his international society into a worldwide confederation of *āśramas,* schools, temples, and farm communities. He passed away in 1977 in Vṛndāvana, India, the place most sacred to Lord Kṛṣṇa. His disciples are carrying forward the movement he started.

Kṛṣṇa
the Reservoir of Pleasure

Kṛṣṇa—this sound is transcendental. Kṛṣṇa means the highest pleasure. Each of us, every living being, seeks pleasure. But we do not know how to seek pleasure perfectly. With a materialistic concept of life, we are frustrated at every step in satisfying our pleasure because we have no information

regarding the real level on which to have real pleasure. To enjoy real pleasure, one must first understand that he is not the body but consciousness. Not exactly consciousness, for consciousness is actually the symptom of our real identity: we are pure soul, now merged within this material body. Modern material science lays no stress on this; therefore the scientists are sometimes misled in their understanding of spirit soul. But spirit soul is a fact, which anyone can understand by the presence of consciousness. Any child can understand that consciousness is the symptom of the spirit soul.

Now the whole process we are trying to learn from the *Bhagavad-gītā* (The Song of God) is how to bring ourselves to this level of consciousness. And if we act from that level of consciousness; then we may not be pushed again into the level of this bodily consciousness, then, at the end of this body we shall be free from material contamination, our spiritual life will be revived, and the ultimate result will be that in our next life, after leaving this body, we shall have our full, eternal spiritual life. Spirit, as we have already discussed, is described as eternal.

Even after the destruction of this body, consciousness is not destroyed. Rather, consciousness is transferred to another type of body and again makes us aware of the material conception of life. That is also described in the *Bhagavad-gītā*. At the time of death, if our consciousness is pure, we can be sure that our next life will not be material—our next life will be spiritual. If our consciousness is not pure at the point of death, then, after leaving this body, we shall have to take another material body. That is the process which is going on. That is nature's law.

We have now a finite body. The body which we see is the gross body. It is just like a shirt and coat: within the coat there is a shirt, and within the shirt there is a body. Similarly, the pure soul is covered by a shirt and coat. The garments are the mind, intelligence and false ego. False ego means the misconception that I am matter, that I am a product of this material world. This misconception makes me localized. For example, because I have taken my birth in India, I think myself Indian. Because I have taken my birth in America, I think myself American. But as pure soul, I am neither Indian nor American. I am pure soul. These others are designations. American, or Indian, or German, or Englishman; cat or dog, or bee or bat, man or wife: all these are designations. In spiritual consciousness we become free from all such designations. That freedom is achieved when we are constantly in touch with the supreme spirit, Kṛṣṇa.

The International Society for Krishna Consciousness is simply intended to keep us in constant touch with Kṛṣṇa. Kṛṣṇa can be in constant companionship with us because He is omnipotent. Therefore, He can be fully in touch with us by His words. His words and He are not different. That is omnipotence. Omnipotence means that everything relating to Him has the same potency. For example, here in this material world, if we are thirsty and we want water, simply repeating "water, water, water, water," will not satisfy our thirst, because this word has not the same potency as water itself. We require the water in substance. Then our thirst will be satisfied.

But in the transcendental, absolute world, there is no such difference—Kṛṣṇa's name, Kṛṣṇa's quality, Kṛṣṇa's word—everything is Kṛṣṇa and provides the same satisfaction.

Some people argue that Arjuna was talking with Kṛṣṇa because Kṛṣṇa was present before him, whereas in my case, Kṛṣṇa is not present. So how can I get directions? But Kṛṣṇa is present by His words—the *Bhagavad-gītā*. In India, when we speak on the *Bhagavad-gītā* or *Śrīmad-Bhāgavatam,* we regularly perform worship with flowers, or with other paraphernalia, as is required for worshiping. In the Sikh religion also, although they have no form of the Deity, they worship the book *Granthasahib*. Perhaps some of you are acquainted with this Sikh community. They worship this *Grantha*. Similarly, the Moslems worship the *Koran*. Similarly, in the Christian world, the *Bible* is worshiped. It is a fact that the Lord Jesus Christ is present by his words. Kṛṣṇa is also present by His words.

These personalities, either God or the son of God, who come from the transcendental world, keep their transcendental identities without being contaminated by the material world. That is their omnipotence. We are in the habit of saying that God is omnipotent. Omnipotence means that He is not different from His name, from His quality, from His pastimes, from His instruction. Therefore, the discussion of *Bhagavad-gītā* is as good as discussion with Kṛṣṇa Himself.

Kṛṣṇa is seated in your heart, and in my heart too. *Īśvaraḥ sarva-bhūtānāṁ hṛd-deśe 'rjuna tiṣṭhati.* God is situated in everyone's heart. God is not away from us. He is present. He is so friendly that He remains with us in our repeated change of births. He is waiting to see when we shall turn to Him. He is so kind that though we may forget Him, He never forgets us. Although a son may forget his father, a father never forgets his son. Similarly, God, the original father of everything, everybody, all living entities, will never forsake us. We may have different bodies, but they are our shirt-coats. That has nothing to do with our real identity. Our real identity is pure soul, and that soul is part and parcel of the Supreme Lord. There are 8,400,000 species of life. Even the biologist and the anthropologist cannot calculate this accurately, but from authoritative, revealed scripture we get this information. Human beings represent 400,000 species, and there are 8,000,000 other species. But Kṛṣṇa, the Supreme Lord, claims that all of them, whether beast, man, snake, god, semi-god, demigod—anything whatever—all of them are, in reality, His sons.

The father gives the seed, and the mother receives the seed. The body is formed, according to the mother's body. And when the body is completely formed, it comes out—either from cats, from dogs, or from man. That is the process of generation. The father gives the seed, and it is emulsified with two kinds of secretion in the womb of the mother, and on the first night the body is formed just like a pea. Then, gradually, it develops. There are nine holes that develop: two ears, two eyes, nostrils, a mouth, a navel, a penis, and an anus.

According to his past *karma,* or action, one gets this body to enjoy or to suffer. That is the process of birth and death. And after finishing this life, again one dies, and again one enters into the womb of some mother. Another type of body then comes out. This is the process of reincarnation.

We should be very diligent as to how we can discontinue this process of repeated birth and death and change of body. That is the prerogative of the human form of life. We can stop this process of repeated change through birth and death. We can get our actual spiritual form again and be blissful, full of knowledge and have eternal life. That is the purpose of evolution. We should not miss this. The entire process of liberation begins just as we have now begun this chanting and hearing. I wish to point out that this chanting of the holy name of God (HARE KRSNA, HARE KRSNA, KRSNA KRSNA, HARE HARE/ HARE RĀMA, HARE RĀMA, RĀMA RĀMA, HARE HARE) and hearing the truths of the *Gītā* is as good as bodily association with Krsna. That is stated in the *Gītā*. This process is called *kīrtana*. Even if one does not understand the language, still, just by hearing, he acquires some piety. His assets lead him to a pious life, even if he does not understand—it has such power.

There are two topics concerning Krsna. Two kinds of topics, actually. One topic is this *Bhagavad-gītā*. It is spoken by Krsna. And the other topic concerning Krsna is *Śrīmad-Bhāgavatam*. That is spoken about Krsna. So there are two types of Krsna *kathā* (topics), and both of them are equally potent because they are connected with Krsna.

Because the *Bhagavad-gītā* is spoken on the Battlefield of Kuruksetra, some people have asked what we have to do with the battlefield. We have nothing to do with any battlefield. We are after knowledge of the spiritual sphere. Then, why should we bother about this battlefield? Because Krsna is on the battlefield, and therefore the whole battlefield has become Krsna-ized. Just as when an electric current is passed into some metal, the whole metal becomes surcharged with electricity; so too, when Krsna is interested in some matter, that matter becomes Krsna-ized. Otherwise, there would be no need of discussing the Battlefield of Kuruksetra. That is His omnipotence.

This omnipotence is also described in *Śrīmad-Bhāgavatam*. There are many Krsna *kathās*. The Vedic literature is full of them. *Vedas* means that they are Krsna *kathās*. Scripture, including the *Vedas*, may appear to be different, but they are all meant for Krsna *kathā*. If we simply hear these topics on Krsna, then what will be the result? It is pure transcendental vibration, and the result will be spiritual consciousness.

We have accumulated many inauspicious things within our hearts due to our material contamination during the course of many, many births. Many, many births—not only this birth, but past births as well. So, when we search into our hearts with the Krsna *kathā*, then the contamination we have accumulated will be washed off. Our hearts will be cleansed of all rubbish. And, as soon as all the rubbish is cleared off, then we are situated in pure consciousness.

It is very difficult to eradicate all the false designations from oneself. For example, I am Indian. It is not very easy to immediately think that I am not Indian, but pure soul. Similarly, it is not a very easy task for anyone to end his identification with these bodily designations. But still, if we continue hearing the Kṛṣṇa *kathā,* it will be very easy. Make an experiment. Make an experiment to see how easily you'll be able to free yourself from all these designations. Of course, it is not possible to clear out the rubbish from the mind all of a sudden, but we are immediately aware that the influence of the material nature has become slackened.

The material nature is working in three modes—goodness, passion and ignorance. Ignorance is hopeless life. Passion is materialistic. One who is influenced by the modes of passion wants this false enjoyment of material existence. Because he does not know the truth, he wants to squeeze out the energy of the body just to enjoy this matter. That is called the mode of passion. As for those in the mode of ignorance, they have neither passion nor goodness. They are in the deepest darkness of life. Situated in the mode of goodness, we can understand, at least theoretically, what I am, what this world is, what God is, and what our interrelationship is. This is the mode of goodness.

By hearing Kṛṣṇa *kathā,* we will be freed from the stages of ignorance and passion. We will be situated in the mode of goodness. At least we'll have the real knowledge—knowledge of what we are. Ignorance is like the animal existence. The animal's life is full of suffering, but the animal does not know that he is suffering. Take the case of a hog. Of course, here in New York, no hog is seen. But in villages in India one sees the hog. Oh, how miserable his life is, living in a filthy place, eating stools and always unclean. Yet the hog is very happy by eating stools, and having constant sexual intercourse with the she-hog and just getting fat. The hog gets very fat, because of the spirit of enjoyment which is there, although, for him, it is sensual enjoyment.

We should not be like the hog, falsely thinking that we are very happy. Working hard all day and night, then having some sex life—we think that in this way we are very happy. But this is not happiness. This has been described in the *Bhāgavatam* as a hog's happiness. Man's happiness is when he is situated in the mode of goodness. Then he can understand what true happiness is.

In our daily routine, if we hear this Kṛṣṇa *kathā*, the result will be that all the dirty things in the heart, accumulated life after life, will be cleared out. As a matter of fact, we will see that we are no longer in ignorance or in passion, but are situated in the mode of goodness. What is that position?

We will find ourselves joyful in every circumstance of life. We will never feel morose. In the *Bhagavad-gītā* we find that this is our *brahma-bhūta* (highest stage of goodness) situation. The *Vedas* teach us that we are not this matter. We are Brahman. *Ahaṁ brahmāsmi.* Lord Śaṅkarācārya preached this gospel to the world. We are not this matter; we are Brahman, spirit. When spiritual realization is actually accomplished, then our symptoms will change. What are those symptoms? When one is situated in his own spiritual consciousness, then he will have no hankering and no lamentation. Lamentation is for loss, and hankering is for gain. Two diseases characterize this material world: what we do not possess, we hanker after, "If I get these things I'll be happy. I have no money, but if I get a million dollars, then I'll be happy." And when we have a million dollars, somehow it will be lost. So we'll cry, "Oh, I have lost it!" When we hanker for earning, that is a kind of distress. And when we suffer loss, that is also distress. But if we are situated in *brahma-bhūta,* we will neither be distressed nor will we hanker. We will view equally everyone and everything. Even if we are situated in the midst of fiery turbulence, we will not be disturbed. That is the mode of goodness.

Bhāgavatam means the science of God. If one perseveres in the science of God, he will be situated in the *brahma-bhūta* status. From that *brahma-bhūta* status, we have to work, for work is recommended here. So long as we have this material body, we have to work. We cannot stop working; it is not possible. But we have to adopt the tactics of *yoga,* and in this way, even by doing some ordinary work, which, by destiny or circumstances we are put into, there is no harm. Suppose that, in one's own occupation, one must speak a lie or his business can't go on. Lying is not a very good thing, so one concludes that the business is not based on very moral principles and one should therefore give it up. In the *Bhagavad-gītā,* however, we find instruction not to give it up. Even if we are put in such circumstances that our livelihood cannot go on without some unfair practice, we should not give it up. But we should try to make it purified. How is it purified? We should not take the fruitive result of our work. That is meant for God.

Sukṛta means pious activities. And *duṣkṛta* means impious activities. On the material level we can be pious or impious. Either we are performing some pious activities, or we are performing some impious activities—or we have a mixture, pious and impious. Lord Kṛṣṇa advises that we should act with knowledge of, or devotion to the Supreme. What does that knowledge mean? It means that I am the part and parcel of the supreme consciousness, or that I am not this body. If I identify myself as an American, as an Indian, or this or that, then I am on the material plane. We should identify ourselves as neither Americans nor Indians, but as pure consciousness. I am a subordinate consciousness of the supreme consciousness; in other words, I am the servant of God. God is the supreme consciousness, and I am His servant. So, for our present understanding, subordinate means servant.

We don't ordinarily carry out the work of a servant in relationship to God. Nobody wants to be a servant, but everyone wants to be the master, because to become a servant is not a very palatable thing. But to become the servant of God is not exactly like this. Sometimes the servant of God becomes the master of God. The real position of the living entity is to be the servant of God, but in the *Bhagavad-gītā* we can see that the master, Kṛṣṇa, became the servant of Arjuna. Arjuna is sitting in the chariot, and Kṛṣṇa is his driver. Arjuna is not the owner of the chariot, but in the spiritual relationship we should not cling to the concept of the material relationship. Although the whole relationship, just as we have experience of it in this world, is there in the spiritual world, that relationship is not contaminated by matter. Therefore it is pure and transcendental. It is of a different nature. As we become advanced in the spiritual conception of life, we can understand what the actual position in the spiritual, transcendental world is.

Here the Lord instructs us in *buddhi-yoga*. *Buddhi-yoga* means that we have full consciousness that we are not this body; and if I act with this understanding, then I am not body—I am consciousness. That is a fact. Now, if we act on the level of consciousness, then we can overcome the fruitive result of good work or bad work. It is a transcendental stage.

It means that we are acting on another's account—on the Supreme's account. We are not liable to loss or gain. When there is gain, we should not be puffed up. We should think, "This gain is for the Lord." And when there is loss, we should know that this is not our responsibility. It is God's work—His. Then we will be happy. This we have to practice: everything on account of the Supreme. This transcendental nature we have to develop. This is the trick of doing work under these present circumstances. As soon as we work on the level of bodily consciousness, we become bound by the reaction of our work. But when we work through spiritual consciousness, we are not bound either by pious activities or by vicious activities. That is the technique.

Manīṣiṇaḥ—this word is very significant. *Manīṣī* means thoughtful. Unless one is thoughtful, he cannot understand that he is not this body. But if one is a little thoughtful he can understand, "Oh, I am not this body. I am consciousness." Sometimes, in our leisure time, we can see, "Oh, this is my finger, and this is my hand. This is my ear, and this is my nose. Everything is mine, but what am I, what am I?" I am feeling this is mine, and that I am. Simply a little thought is required. Everything is mine—my eyes, my finger, my hand. My, my, my, and what is the I? The I is that consciousness, in which I am thinking, "This is mine."

Now, if I am not this body, then why should I act for this body? I should act for myself. Then, how can I work for myself? What is my position? I am consciousness. But what kind of consciousness? Subordinate consciousness—I am part of the supreme consciousness. Then, what will my activities be? My activities will be under the guidance of the supreme consciousness, just as in the office, the managing director is the supreme consciousness. For example, in the office everyone is working under the direction of the manager; therefore they have no responsibility. They have only to discharge their duties. Either pious or impious duties—never mind. In the military line, too, the order of the captain or commander is there. The soldier has to execute it. He does not consider whether it is pious or impious. That does not matter. He simply has to act; then he is a real soldier. He acts in that way and he gets his reward. He gets title and honor. He doesn't care. The commander says, "Just go and kill the enemy," and he is rewarded. Do you think that by killing one gets reward? No—it is for the duty discharged.

Similarly, here the situation is that Kṛṣṇa is instructing Arjuna. Kṛṣṇa is the supreme consciousness. I am consciousness, the part and parcel of the supreme consciousness. So my duty is to act according to that supreme consciousness. For example, I consider my hand as a part of my body. Now, it is moving in its own way. "As I want, let my hand be moved. Let my legs be moved. Let my eyes be opened and see." So, I am dictating, and these parts are working. Similarly, we are all parts and parcels of the Supreme. When we train ourselves to move and act in accordance with supreme consciousness, then we become transcendental to all these pious or impious activities. That is the technique. What will the result of this technique be? We become free from the bondage of birth and death. No more birth and death.

Modern scientists and philosophers do not think about these four things: birth, death, disease and old age. They set them aside. "Oh, let us be happy. Let us enjoy this life." But human life is meant for finding a solution to this bondage of birth, death, disease and old age. If any civilization has not found a solution to these four problems, then that is not a human civilization. Human civilization is meant for finding a complete solution to these things.

So here in the *Bhagavad-gītā*, the Lord says, *karma-jaṁ buddhi-yuktāḥ*. *Karma-jaṁ* means whenever there is action there will be some reaction. If one acts in badness, there will be a bad reaction. But reaction, either good or bad, is, in the higher sense, all suffering. Suppose that by good action I get a good birth, fine bodily features and a good education. All these good things I may have, but that does not mean that I am free from material pains. The material pains are birth, death, old age and disease. Even if I am a rich man, a beautiful man, an educated man, born in an aristocratic family, etc., I still cannot avoid death, old age and disease.

So, we must not be concerned with pious activities or impious activities. We must be concerned with transcendental activities only. That will save us from this bondage of birth, death, old age and disease. That should be our aim in life. We should not be hankering after good or bad things. For example, suppose one is suffering from some disease. He is lying in bed, eating, passing nature's call uncomfortably, taking bitter medicines. He always has to be kept clean by the nurses; otherwise there is an obnoxious smell. While he is lying in this condition some friends come to him and ask how he is feeling. "Yes, I am feeling well." What is this well? Lying in bed uncomfortably taking bitter medicine, and unable to move! Yet despite all these inconveniences he says, "I am well." Similarly, in our material conception of life, if we think, "I am happy," that is foolishness. There is no happiness in material life. It is impossible to have happiness here. In this condition, we do not know the meaning of happiness. That's why this very word is used—*manīṣiṇaḥ*—thoughtful.

We seek happiness by some extraneous, artificial means, but how long does it last? It will not endure. We again come back to sorrow. Suppose, by intoxication, we feel happy. That is not our actual happiness. Suppose I am made unconscious by chloroform, and I don't feel the pain of an operation. That does not mean that I am not having an operation. This is artificial. Real pleasure, real life exists.

As is commanded in the *Bhagavad-gītā* by Śrī Kṛṣṇa, the thoughtful give up the reaction of work, being situated on the level of pure consciousness. The result is that this bondage of birth and death, disease and old age comes to an end. This end is in union with the true identity, Kṛṣṇa, the reservoir of pleasure and eternal bliss. There, indeed, is the true happiness for which we are intended.

Kṛṣṇa the Supreme Lovable Object

from *THE NECTAR OF DEVOTION*

Bhakti means devotional service. Every service has some attractive feature which drives the servitor progressively on and on. Everyone of us within this world is perpetually engaged in some sort of service, and the impetus for such service is the pleasure we derive from it. Driven by affection for his wife and children, a family man works day and night. A philanthropist works in the same way for love of the greater family, and a nationalist for the cause of his country and countrymen.

That force which drives the philanthropist, the householder and the nationalist is called *rasa,* or a kind of mellow (relationship) whose taste is very sweet. *Bhakti-rasa* is a mellow different from the ordinary *rasa* enjoyed by mundane workers. Mundane workers labor very hard day and night in order to relish a certain kind of *rasa* which is understood as sense gratification. The relish or taste of the mundane *rasa* does not endure, and therefore mundane workers are always apt to change their position of enjoyment. A businessman is not satisfied by working the whole week; therefore, wanting a change for the weekend, he goes to a place where he tries to forget his business activities. Then, after the weekend is spent in forgetfulness, he again changes his position and resumes his actual business activities. Material engagement means accepting a particular status for some time and then changing it. This position of changing back and forth is technically known as *bhoga-tyāga,* which means a position of alternating sense enjoyment and renunciation. A living entity cannot steadily remain either in sense enjoyment or in renunciation. A change is going on perpetually, and we cannot be happy in either state because of our eternal constitutional position of being eternal fragmental parts of the Supreme Lord.

Sense gratification does not endure for long, and it is therefore called *capala-sukha,* or flickering happiness. For example, an ordinary family man who works very hard day and night and is successful in giving comforts to the members of his family thereby relishes a kind of mellow, but his whole advancement of material happiness immediately terminates along with his body as soon as his life is over. Death is therefore taken as the representative of God for the atheistic class of man. The devotee realizes the presence of God by devotional service, whereas the atheist realizes the presence of God in the shape of death. At death everything is finished, and one has to begin a new chapter of life in a new situation, perhaps higher or lower than the last one. In any field of activity, political, social, national or international, the result of our actions will be finished with the end of life. That is sure.

Bhakti-rasa, however, the mellow relished in the transcendental loving service of the Lord, does not finish with the end of life. It continues perpetually and is therefore called *amṛta,* that which does not die but exists eternally. This is confirmed in all Vedic literatures. The *Bhagavad-gītā* says that a little advancement in *bhakti-rasa* can save the devotee from the greatest danger, that of missing the opportunity for human life. The *rasas* derived from our feelings in social life, in family life, or in the greater family life of altruism, philanthropism, nationalism, socialism, communism, etc., do not guarantee that one's next life will be as a human being. We prepare our next life by our actual activities in the present life. A living entity is offered a particular type of body as a result of his action in the present body.

The basic principle of the living condition is that we have a general propensity to love someone. No one can live without loving someone else. This propensity is present in every living being. Even an animal like a tiger has this loving propensity at least in a dormant stage, and it is certainly present in the human beings. The missing point, however, is where to repose our love so that everyone can become happy. At the present moment the human society teaches one to love his country or family or his personal self, but there is no information where to repose the loving propensity so that everyone can become happy. That missing point is Kṛṣṇa, and the process of devotional service teaches us how to stimulate our original love for Kṛṣṇa and how to be situated in that position where we can enjoy our blissful life.

In the primary stage a child loves his parents, then his brothers and sisters, and as he daily grows up he begins to love his family, society, community, country, nation, or even the whole human society. But the loving propensity is not satisfied even by loving all human society; that loving propensity remains imperfectly fulfilled until we know who is the supreme beloved. Our love can be fully satisfied only when it is reposed

in Kṛṣṇa. This theme is the sum and substance of the science of Kṛṣṇa consciousness, which teaches us how to love Kṛṣṇa in five devotional transcendental mellows.

Our loving propensity expands just as a vibration of light or air expands, but we do not know where it ends. *Bhakti-yoga* teaches us the science of loving every one of the living entities perfectly by the easy method of loving Kṛṣṇa. We have failed to create peace and harmony in human society, even by such great attempts as the United Nations, because we do not know the right method. The method is very simple, but one has to understand it with a cool head. *The Nectar of Devotion* teaches all men how to perform the simple and natural method of loving Kṛṣṇa, the Supreme Personality of Godhead. If we learn how to love Kṛṣṇa, then it is very easy to immediately and simultaneously love every living being. It is like pouring water on the root of a tree or supplying food to one's stomach. The method of pouring water on the root of a tree or supplying foodstuffs to the stomach is universally scientific and practical, as every one of us has experienced. Everyone knows well that when we eat something, or in other words when we put foodstuffs in the stomach, the energy created by such action is immediately distributed throughout the whole body. Similarly, when we pour water on the root, the energy thus created is immediately distributed throughout the entirety of even the largest tree. It is not possible to water the tree part by part, nor is it possible to feed the different parts of the body separately. *The Nectar of Devotion* will teach us how to turn the one switch that will immediately brighten everything, everywhere. One who does not know this method is missing the point of life.

As far as material necessities are concerned, the human civilization at the present moment is very much advanced in living comfortably, but we are still not happy because we are missing the point. The material comforts of life alone are not sufficient to make us happy. The vivid example is America: The richest nation of the world, having all facilities for material comfort, is producing a class of men completely confused and frustrated in life. I am appealing herewith to such confused men to learn the art of devotional service, as directed explicitly in *The Nectar of Devotion,* and I am sure that the fire of material existence burning within their hearts will be immediately extinguished. The root cause of our dissatisfaction is that our dormant loving propensity has not been fulfilled despite our great advancement in the materialistic way of life. This transcendental science will

the Supreme Lovable Object

give us practical hints as to how we can live in this material world perfectly engaged in devotional service and thus fulfill all our desires in this life and the next. This knowledge is not presented to condemn any way of materialistic life, but the attempt is to give information to religionists, philosophers and people in general how to love Kṛṣṇa. One may live without material discomfiture, but at the same time he should learn the art of loving Kṛṣṇa.

At the present moment we are inventing so many ways to utilize our propensity to love, but factually we are missing the real point, Kṛṣṇa. We are watering all parts of the tree but missing the tree's root. We are trying to keep our body fit by all means, but we are neglecting to supply foodstuffs to the stomach.

Missing Kṛṣṇa means missing one's self also. Real self-realization and realization of Kṛṣṇa go together simultaneously. For example, seeing oneself in the morning means seeing the sunrise also; without seeing the sunshine no one can see himself. Similarly, unless one has realized Kṛṣṇa there is no question of self-realization.

Lord Śrī Kṛṣṇa Caitanya Mahāprabhu, who was Kṛṣṇa Himself, appeared 485 years ago in Bengal and gave us the process for attaining pure love of God in this age. Simply by constantly chanting and hearing the transcendental sound vibration Hare Kṛṣṇa, Hare Kṛṣṇa, Kṛṣṇa Kṛṣṇa, Hare Hare/ Hare Rāma, Hare Rāma, Rāma Rāma, Hare Hare, one can achieve the desired goal of life.

We invite all people of all colors, of all creeds and of all walks of life to come and join us in chanting this Hare Kṛṣṇa *mahāmantra* and experience its transcendental potency. Anyone of any religion who takes up this process of God realization, Kṛṣṇa consciousness, will develop his love of God and thereby perfect his life.

The Perfect

Kṛṣṇa consciousness is a very important movement meant to bring all living entities back to their original consciousness. Just as there are many mental hospitals like Bellevue, established for the purpose of bringing a crazy man back to his original consciousness, similarly the purpose of this Kṛṣṇa consciousness movement is to bring all crazy men back to their original consciousness.

Anyone who is not Kṛṣṇa conscious may be understood to be more or less crazy. There was a murder case in India in which a murderer pleaded that he had become mad and therefore did not know what he did. So in order to test him to see whether he was actually a lunatic at that time, the expert civil psychiatrist was brought to examine him. The doctor gave his opinion saying that he had studied many cases, and all the patients with whom he had come in contact were more or less crazy, and the court could excuse him on those grounds if it desired. In a Bengali poem a great Vaiṣṇava poet has written, "When a man becomes haunted by ghosts, he speaks only nonsense. Similarly, anyone who is under the influence of material nature is haunted, and whatever he speaks is nonsense." Although one is a great philosopher or a great scientist, if he is haunted by the ghost of *māyā*, illusion, whatever he theorizes and whatever he speaks is more or less nonsense.

The intent of this movement is to bring such a man back to his original consciousness, which is Kṛṣṇa consciousness, clear consciousness. When water falls from the clouds, it is like distilled water—without contamination. But as soon as it touches the ground it becomes muddy and colored. Similarly, we are spirit soul, part and parcel of Kṛṣṇa, and therefore our

Person

original constitutional position is as pure as God's. In *Bhagavad-gītā* it is stated, *mamaivāṁśo jīva-loke:* the living entities are part and parcel of Kṛṣṇa (Bg. 15.7). As a fragment of gold is gold, so, similarly, we are minute particles of God's body and are therefore qualitatively as good as God. The chemical composition of God's body and our body (not the material body but our spiritual body) is the same, and thus ours is as good as God's, for the chemical composition is one. But as rain water falls down to the ground, so we come in contact with this material world, the material nature, which is manipulated by the material energy of Kṛṣṇa.

When we speak of nature, it must be inquired, "Whose nature?"God's nature. Nature is not active independently. Such a concept is foolish. In *Bhagavad-gītā* it is clearly said that material nature is not independent. A foolish man sees a machine and thinks that it is working automatically, but actually it is not—there is a driver, although we sometimes cannot see the driver behind the machine due to our defective vision. There are electronic machines working very wonderfully, but behind the electronics there must be a scientist who pushes the button. This is very simple to understand. Since a machine is matter, it cannot work on its own accord but must work under spiritual direction. A tape recorder works, but it works under the direction of a living entity, a human being. The machine is complete, but unless it is manipulated by a spirit soul it cannot work. Similarly, we should take it for granted that the cosmic manifestation of nature is a great machine; but behind this material nature there is God, Kṛṣṇa.

Kṛṣṇa says in *Bhagavad-gītā, mayādhyakṣeṇa prakṛtiḥ sūyate sacarācaram:* "All material nature is acting under My direction and superintendence." (Bg. 9.10) There are two kinds of entities—the moving (such as human beings, animals and ants) and non-moving (such as trees and mountains). Kṛṣṇa says that material nature, which controls both kinds of entities, is acting under His direction. There is a supreme control. Modern civilization does not understand this due to lack of knowledge, so our Kṛṣṇa consciousness movement is trying to enlighten people. People are all crazy because they are conducted by the influence of the three modes of material nature. They are not in their normal condition.

There are so many universities, especially in the United States, and so many departments of knowledge—why aren't they discussing these points? Where is the department for this knowledge? In 1968, when I went to Boston and was invited to speak at Massachusetts Institute of Technology, my first question was, "Where is the technological department which is investigating the difference between a dead man and a living man?" When a man dies, something is lost. Where is the technology to replace it? Why do the scientists not try for it? Because this is a very difficult subject, they set it aside. They are busily engaged in the technology of eating, sleeping, mating and defending. This is animal technology. Animals are also trying their best to eat nicely, to have nice sex life, to sleep, and to defend. What is the difference between man's knowledge and animal knowledge? Man's knowledge should be developed to explore the technology which deals with the difference between a living man and a dead man, a living body and a dead body. That spiritual knowledge was taught by Kṛṣṇa in the beginning of *Bhagavad-gītā*. Arjuna was talking to Kṛṣṇa as a friend. Of course, whatever he was saying was right, but it was right only to a certain point. Beyond that point there are other subject matters of knowledge, which are called *adhokṣaja* because our direct perception of material knowledge fails to approach them. We have many powerful microscopes to see what we cannot see with our limited vision, but there is no microscope that can show us the soul within the body. But nevertheless the soul is there.

Bhagavad-gītā informs us that within this body there is a proprietor. I am the proprietor of my body, and others are the proprietors of their bodies. I say "my hand." I don't say "I hand." Therefore, since it is "my hand," I am different from this hand. When I say "my book," this indicates that the book is different from me. Similarly, it is "my table," "my eye," "my leg," "my this," "my that"—but where am I? Searching out the answer to this question is meditation. One asks, "Where am I? What am I?" We cannot search out the answers to such questions by material effort. Therefore all the universities are setting this aside: "It is a very difficult subject." Engineers are very proud of creating the horseless carriage. Formerly horses were drawing carriages, but now there are cars, so the scientists are very proud. "We have invented horseless carriages and wingless birds," they say. They can invent imitation wings for the airplane, but when they invent a soulless body, then they will deserve credit. Such an invention cannot be, for no machine can work without a soul. Even computers need trained men to handle them. Similarly, we should understand that this great machine known as the cosmic manifestation or material nature is manipulated by a supreme spirit. That is Kṛṣṇa. Scientists are searching for the ultimate cause or the ultimate controller of this material nature and are putting forth different theories and propositions, but our means of knowledge is very easy and perfect because we are hearing from the perfect person, Kṛṣṇa. Because Kṛṣṇa says so, we immediately know that the cosmic machine, of which the earth is part, is working so nicely and wonderfully because behind this machine is a driver—Kṛṣṇa. Exactly as behind any machine there is a machine driver, similarly, behind this big machine of material nature there is Kṛṣṇa.

Our process of knowledge is very easy. Kṛṣṇa's book, *Bhagavad-gītā*, is the book of knowledge which is given by the perfect person. One may argue that although we have accepted Him as a perfect person, others do not; but He is the perfect person on the evidence of many authorities. It is not by our whims that we accept Kṛṣṇa as perfect. No—there are many Vedic authorities like Vyāsadeva, the author of all Vedic literature. The treasure house of knowledge is contained in the *Vedas*, and their author, Vyāsadeva, accepts Kṛṣṇa as the Supreme Personality of Godhead. His spiritual master, Nārada, accepts Kṛṣṇa as the Supreme Personality of Godhead and his spiritual master, Brahmā, accepts Kṛṣṇa as the Supreme Person. Brahmā says, *īśvaraḥ paramaḥ kṛṣṇaḥ*: "The supreme controller is Kṛṣṇa."

No one can say that he is without a controller. That is not possible. Everyone, no matter how big an officer he is, has a controller over his head. But Kṛṣṇa has no controller; therefore He is God. He is the controller of everyone, but He has no controller. There are many so-called gods nowadays. Gods have become very cheap. They are especially imported from India. People in other countries are fortunate that gods are not manufactured there, but in India gods are manufactured practically every day. One of my disciples recently told me that a god was coming to Los Angeles and that people were requested to receive him. Kṛṣṇa is not that kind of god. I mentioned in my introduction to *Kṛṣṇa Book* that Kṛṣṇa is not the type of god manufactured in a mystic factory. No. He is God. He was not made God, but He is God.

Behind the gigantic material nature, the cosmic manifestation, there is God—Kṛṣṇa—and He is accepted by all authorities. We must accept that knowledge which is accepted by authorities. For education we go to a teacher or to a school or learn from our father and mother. They are all authorities, and our nature is to learn from them. In our childhood, we asked, "Father, what is this?" Father would say, "This is a pen," "These are spectacles," or "This is a table." So a child learns from his father and mother—"This is a table, these are spectacles, this is a pen, this is my sister, this is my brother, etc." Similarly, if we get information from an authority and if the authority is not a cheater, then our knowledge is perfect. The father and mother never cheat when the son inquires from them, and they give exact and correct information. If we get the right information from the right person, that is perfect knowledge. If we want to reach the conclusion by speculation, that is imperfect. The inductive process will never become perfect. It will always remain imperfect.

Since we get information from the perfect person, Kṛṣṇa, whatever we speak is perfect. I don't say anything which is not spoken by Kṛṣṇa or by authorities who have accepted Kṛṣṇa. That is called disciplic succession. That is Kṛṣṇa consciousness. In *Bhagavad-gītā* Kṛṣṇa recommends this process of knowledge (*evaṁ paramparā-prāptam imaṁ rājarṣayo viduḥ*). (Bg. 4.2) Formerly knowledge was passed down by great saintly kings who were the authorities. Nowadays the government or president is the authority. Formerly, however, those authorities or kings were *ṛṣis*—great learned scholars and devotees, not ordinary men. That system of government was very nice. One talented and well trained person as the head of the government could very peacefully execute the governmental functions. There are many instances in Vedic civilization of the perfection of such kings. Dhruva Mahārāja is such an example. He went to the forest to search out God, and by practice of severe penance and austerities he found God within six months. How? He was a five-year-old boy, a king's son with a very delicate body, but according to the direction of his spiritual master, Nārada, he went alone to the forest. The first month there he simply ate some fruits and vegetables every three days. For the next three months he drank a little water every six days. For the next month, he would inhale some air every twelve days. For six whole months he stood on one leg and executed these austerities, and at the end of six months, God became manifest before him, eye to eye. If we practice austerities, it will be possible for us to also see God eye to eye. This is the perfection of life.

The Kṛṣṇa consciousness movement is based on austerity, but it is not very difficult. We recommend that our students not have illicit sex. We don't stop sex, but we regulate it. We don't stop eating, but we regulate it; we eat Kṛṣṇa *prasādam*, food first offered to Kṛṣṇa. We don't say, "no eating," but "no meat-eating." What is the difficulty? Kṛṣṇa *prasādam* is made of many varieties of nicely cooked fruits and vegetables, so there is no

difficulty. "No illicit sex" means don't be like cats and dogs—be married and have one wife or one husband and be satisfied. We must regulate ourselves and must undergo austerities, although we cannot undergo such severe types of austerity as Dhruva Mahārāja. In these days it is impossible to imitate Dhruva Mahārāja, but the method we are prescribing is possible. If one takes to these principles, he will make advancement in spiritual consciousness, Kṛṣṇa consciousness. As one makes advancement in Kṛṣṇa consciousness, he becomes perfect in knowledge. What is the use of becoming a scientist or a philosopher who cannot say what his next life will be? These students of Kṛṣṇa consciousness can very easily say what their next life is, what God is, what we are and what our relationship with God is. Their knowledge is perfect because they are reading perfect books of knowledge such as *Bhagavad-gītā* and *Śrīmad-Bhāgavatam*.

This is our process. It is very easy, and anyone can adopt it and make his life perfect. If someone says, "I am not educated; I cannot read books," still there is the possibility that he can perfect his life. He can simply chant Hare Kṛṣṇa. Kṛṣṇa has given us a tongue and two ears, and we may be surprised to know that Kṛṣṇa is realized through the tongue, not through the eyes. After the tongue the other senses follow, but the tongue is the chief. We have to control the tongue. How does one control it? Simply chant Hare Kṛṣṇa and taste Kṛṣṇa *prasādam*.

One cannot understand Kṛṣṇa by sensual perception or by speculation. It is not possible, for Kṛṣṇa is so great that He is not within our sensual range. But He can be understood by surrender. Kṛṣṇa therefore recommends this process. *Sarva-dharmān parityajya mām ekaṁ śaraṇaṁ vraja:* "Give up all other processes of religion and simply surrender unto Me." (Bg. 18.66) Our disease is that we are rebellious. We don't want to accept authority. Yet although we say that we don't want authority, nature is so strong that it forces authority upon us. We are forced to accept the authority of nature by our senses. To say that we are independent is nonsense; it is our foolishness. We are under authority, but still we say that we don't want authority. This is called *māyā,* illusion. We do, however, have a certain independence— we can choose to be under the authority of our senses or the authority of Kṛṣṇa. The best and ultimate authority is Kṛṣṇa, for He is our eternal well-wisher, and He always speaks for our benefit. Since we have to accept some authority, why not accept His? Simply by hearing of His glories from *Bhagavad-gītā* and *Śrīmad-Bhāgavatam* and by chanting His names—Hare Kṛṣṇa—we can swiftly perfect our lives.